Gloopy Food

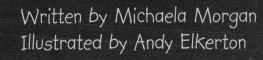

Written by Michaela Morgan
Illustrated by Andy Elkerton

Horribilly is a ...

BIG ...

green and gloopy ...

soggy ...

monster.

He is the only monster at Golden Pond School.

Horribilly has lots of friends.

They have lots of fun at school.

"What do you want to eat?" asked his friends one lunchtime.

Horribilly said,

"Bugs!
I love bugs.
Crispy, crunchy bugs,
big and munchy bugs.
I love bugs."

Everyone said, "YUCK!"

"We'll help you," said his friends.
They gave him ...

one mini pizza,

some fresh salad,

6

two small bananas

and a brown roll.

This did NOT look
like food to Horribilly.
So ...

... he threw the bananas in the air.

He stuck the salad in his hair.

He made a flying frisbee with the pizza.
"Don't be silly, Horribilly!" said his friends.

Then Horribilly put
the pizza on his nose.

He put the brown roll
on his toes.

He put a banana
in each ear and ...

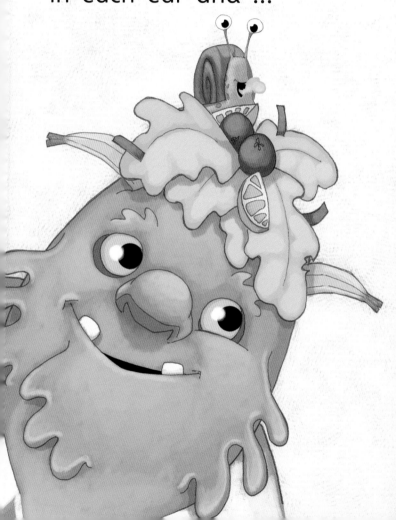

with the roll
he scored a goal!

"Don't play with your food!"
said his friends. "Eat it!"
"It's too dry!" said Horribilly.
"I like gloopy food."

Big, green tears ran down his face.

Then he found out about **tomato sauce**.

Now he loves his school lunch ...

... and he thinks that bananas are yummy!